fear only those

things

that can steal your

soul

and rip it to

pieces

bedtime stories

for

naughty children

Azriel St. Michael

Bedtime Stories for Naughty Children

AZRIEL ST. MICHAEL

BEDTIME STORIES FOR NAUGHTY CHILDREN

Azriel St. Michael

An original publication by Shemyaza Press

FIRST EDITION

Canada

ISBN 978-0-9876921-0-8

Photography by Karen Sopotyk-Pidskalny
At KMP Photography.
Make-up by Tamsen Rae

BEDTIME STOREIS FOR NAUGHTY CHILDREN. © 2011 by Azriel St. Michael. All Rights Reserved. Printed in the United States of America. Published in Canada. No part of this book may be used or reproduced in any manner whatsoever without written permission from the author himself, except in the case of brief quotations embodied in critical articles and reviews. For further information address the publisher at Shemyaza Press, RR5 Site 17 Comp 49 Prince Albert, Sk, Canada. S6v-5r3.

SHEMYAZA PRESS

.A DIVISION OF THE SHEMYAZA SYNDICATE GROUP

Deadication

To the Ones whose lidless eyes stared down into my crib;
The Ones who crept out of my closet in the dead of night;
The Ones who scarred my flesh and marked my soul;
The Ones who showed me the darkest depths of fear,
And the futility of desperate prayers.

Before I learned to sing,
You taught me to scream.

Azriel St. Michael

CONTENTS

"We often forget how much unites all the members of humanity.... some universal alien threat from outside this world."

Ronald Regan,
Speech to the United Nations General Assembly
Sept. 21st, 1987

"I think the kids on this planet are wise to the truth, and I think we ought to give it to them. I think they deserve it."

Colonel Philip Corso,
Army Intelligence officer, former Head of Foreign Technology at the U.S. Army's Research and Development Department at the Pentagon.

"I can therefore see no alternative to accepting the theory that they come from an extraterrestrial source."

Air Chief Marshall Lord Dowding,
Commanding Officer of the RAF during WWII.

"I was not content to believe in a personal devil and serve him. I wanted to get hold of him personally and become his chief of staff."

Aleister Crowley

Introduction

Every year in North America, over one million people are reported missing.

Think about that fact for a moment. Over 2,300 people go missing every single day. Simply put, the equivalent population of Tucson Arizona, or Winnipeg, Manitoba, gone; the entire Province of Saskatchewan, Canada, gone.

You don't hear about it in the news, but if one third of the City of Los Angeles vanished over night, it would be a national crisis. Spread out over the continent, however, these disappearances are less noticeable, but they are no less real.

One person every 35 seconds.

Law enforcement agencies are at a loss to explain it, and strangely, no bodies have yet been found. Many victims were last seen getting ready for bed; then they simply vanished without a trace.

They have never been seen again.

These disturbing facts raise a grim and serious question; What happened to them? We see their pictures every day, in newspapers, on the sides of milk cartons, posted on bulletin boards in shopping malls and grocery stores, and it makes us wonder....

Where did they go?

Who----or what----is silently stalking the bedrooms of our neighbourhoods, preying upon us once we've turned out the lights? As the numbers continue to swell each year, the truth becomes undeniable. We are not just being hunted. Mankind is quietly being exterminated. As absurd as this statement may sound, the unsettling facts speak for themselves.

Scoff if you like, but let me ask you; are you one of those people who crawls into bed every night carefully saying your prayers? Do you wish for pleasant, peaceful dreams, yet dread that final moment when you turn out the lights and find yourself utterly alone? You tug the blankets up tight about you, as if their warmth will somehow keep you safe---

But safe from what?
While shadows linger near you dare not ask nor ponder the import of this question. However, one stark and chilling possibility remains. You might just be the next to disappear----to never be seen again.

Sometimes the sleep you seek comes easily. You wake with the golden dawn spilling in through slitted blinds. The blessed sunrise of a glorious new day burns away troublesome memories of last night's fears.

How soon you forget the strange noises in the dark that robbed you of your rest!
The cruel, unearthly silhouettes, sneering menacingly from the corners of your room as the black of night pressed in upon you.

There are other times, however, when sleep is difficult to find. The bloody hues of sunset fade into a hideous black oblivion. As spiders creep out from cracks in the walls, that uneasy, restless feeling begins to set in. You toss and turn ceaselessly, the blankets pulled up and tucked tightly over your head. And all the while your deepest, darkest fears close in around you like plague flies on a rotting corpse.

You envision them, terrifying, monstrous creatures, fangs dripping venomous slime. Their claws sharp as razors, talons of steel, inching nearer with every ragged breath you take. You pray for them to leave but still they remain, their amber lidless eyes glaring at you with demonic hunger, stalking closer by the second, silent as the ghosts of murdered men.

The fear you feel in those dreadful moments is suffocating, and all too real. Every minute seems like an eternity as your heart pounds feverishly in your chest and your pulse races to the rhythm of certain death.

Go ahead. *Laugh if you like.*
Deny your instinctive fear of the dark----after all, it's so easy to be brave in the light of day, isn't it?

But in the bitter watches of the night, shadows speak. Ghosts and phantoms slither from their graves like angry serpents, and un-dead creatures claw their way out of damp, mouldering tombs to feed upon the warm flesh of the living. In the cold desolation of darkness you realize far beyond any shadow of doubt----

There are dead things that live once the sun has set.

Things that wake once you turn out the lights!

They have been there since before time began. And tonight they will rise again, to lurk just within your room, anxiously awaiting the moment you finally fall asleep. They were born in black, demon-haunted caverns and dungeons, in places were the Devil himself fears to tread. Loathsome beings that venture out into the night, to feast upon helpless, mortal prey.

They are quiet, stealthy and cruel. Their ominous eyes burn like brimstone in the utter void of night. They hide in your closet and under your bed where the damned souls of Hell await, listening to your trembling breath, desperate to satisfy their insatiable, ravenous greed.

Trust me when I tell you now, these demons are all too real.

As real as the fear creeping into your mind; as absolute as the certainty that one day----or night----you will surely die. They are not merely figments of your imagination.

At this moment, as you read these words, they wait somewhere nearby, in the shadows of this very room. They hunger for living flesh and blood, and these terrors all have names.

They are the Hallows.

The Eaters of Dreams and Ashes.

The Eaters of the Dead.

They are soulless.

Devoid of love.

Eternal as the black empty spaces between the stars.

But don't just take my word for it. Dim the lights, and turn the page if you dare.

Let me introduce you to some friends of mine….

"For I say unto you; even the demons in Hell believe.
And They tremble."

Jesus Christ

Do You Believe?

Do you believe in demons?
Did I hear you say no?
You answered rather quickly,
Perhaps you've never known;
The freezing fright at midnight,
When something dead is near;
When all your faith in God and Christ,
Is swallowed by your fear?

I'm not talking 'bout the ghost,
In the hall outside your door;
Nor the shapeless, shifting shadows,
Creeping silent on the floor.
Those are merely dead men,
Awakened from their tombs;
They haven't found their rest yet,
That's why they haunt your room.

I'm talking real, live demons,
Creatures born in Hell.
Spawned in hate and malice,
Amid the sulphurous smell;
Of rotting souls in torment,
Where Angels dare not tread;
In deep, black pits of brimstone,
That lie beneath your bed.

Have you ever seen a demon?
Up close and face to face?
With the bitter darkness crushing in,
As black as a Witch's hate?
With no one there to save you,
No one to hear you scream;
Trapped inside a nightmare,
Too real to be a dream.

Your heart pounding like thunder,
To the rhythm of your death;
With nothing between you and Hell,
Except your terror-stricken breath.
Staring at those yellow eyes,
That glare back ever cruel,
In the end you realize,
That you have been a fool.

Do you believe in demons?
I didn't think so;

But perhaps tonight you will....

All Hallows Eve

Once I stood upon a path
As night fell darkly;
And ghastly clouds assailed the moon
That shone so starkly;
On All Hallows Eve.

Amid a grove of ancient oak
My path wound faintly;
Gaunt and naked, they swayed and spoke
And none too sweetly;
On All Hallows Eve.

A chill wind roused their quaking limbs
As I stood alone;
They voiced a song, a rattled hymn
Freezing blood and bone;
On All Hallows Eve.

A wooden dirge not voiced by men
The ancient grove resounded;
And my heart failed, as on the trail
Unearthly footsteps pounded;
On All Hallows Eve.

I waited there, too scared to move
The night grew blacker;
Amid the tramp of cloven hooves
And devil's laughter;
On All Hallows Eve.

Like damned souls borne on angry seas
Pale mist swirled ahead;
Swarming o'er the rust of leaves
The Long Forgotten Dead;
On All Hallows Eve.

The footsteps ceased; silence now,
Except the oaken groan;
But the sudden still was void of peace
I was not alone;
On All Hallows Eve.

With awesome fright I realised
The Darkness was alive!
With things that should be dead, yet live
Only on one night;
On All Hallows Eve.

I dare not move nor make a sound
Too afraid for breath;
In the bitter black dwell nameless horrors
Even the Angels dread;
On All Hallows Eve.

Ten thousand lidless, loveless eyes
Burning fierce with spite;
Risen from the bowels of Hell
Feeding just one night;
On All Hallows Eve.

Somehow I whispered a frantic prayer
Begging God to hear;
But only Dead men heard my pleas
While slowly creeping near;
On All Hallows Eve.

Suddenly I woke up screaming
Like a butchered saint;
Gasping desperately for breath
Just about to faint;
On All Hallows Eve.

"It was only just a dream!" I laughed aloud
My heartbeat racing wild;
While reaching out to flick the lights on
Feeling like a child;
On All Hallows Eve.

When something roused my fright anew
Swelling now in spades;
A movement caught within the Moonlight
Spilling though the shades;
On All Hallows Eve.

At the foot of my bed sat the Devil himself
Grinning with wicked glee;
"God was busy, so I came instead;
I am always free;
On All Hallows Eve."

The Eaters Of Dreams

Behind the mirror's polished glass,
Lie strange and frightening things;
Far older than the race of man,
A world that has no Dreams.

There within the shadows,
They've lived since Earth was born;
And even now they linger,
Forgotten and forlorn.

Once they ventured forward,
Into the light of day;
They came to feed their hunger,
And then they went away.

For men were mindless creatures,
Evolving from the Sea;
We had no Dreams to offer,
And no nightmares to feed.

They waited through the ages,
The dread Eaters of Dreams;
While men crept from the primal ooze,
Earth blossomed, lush and green.

As our minds began to grow,
So too did our form;
Amid primeval chaos,
Humanity was born.

First we crept up slowly,
From the Ocean's murky depths;
Crawling up the muddy banks,
With timid, reptile, steps.

We had no intuition,
No thought for where we'd been;
But Evolution started,
When we began to dream.

We shed our scales and learned to run,
As we became the prey;
Nameless monsters ruled the land,
And we hid from the day.

Stark eons changed the landscape,
Volcanic ash and stones;
Gave way to steaming jungles,
And there we made our homes.

Soon we were the hunters,
The monsters now our prey;
We started building cities,
And lost our fear of day.

When twilight roused our memories,
Like half forgotten dreams;
We built walls to protect us,
And shut out dreadful things.

Yet we feared the Darkness,
Where stark, grim terrors dwell;
So we invented Mighty Gods,
To save our souls from Hell.

And all the while they waited,
The Eaters of our Dreams;
Festering in shadow lands,
In bitter realms unseen.

Soon we ruled the whole Earth,
We conquered Air and Sea;
The Ancient Gods abandoned,
Our faith placed in machines.

We scoffed at our past terrors,
Choosing to believe;
Only in the daylight,
And things our eyes could see.

Now we live in comfort,
We think there's naught to fear;
We go to bed and think we're safe,
Forgetful of the Mirror.

And while we slumber they creep out,
The Eaters of our Dreams;
Lurking in the shadows,
Morose and bitter Beings.

Burning now with hatred,
They steal into our rooms
Twisted, angry, soulless fiends,
Intent upon our doom.

They come because they hunger,
They come 'cause we forget;
That when our Dreams have ended,
We draw our final breath.

Creeping ever nearer,
While we sleep unawares;
They steal our Dreams and eat them,
Then hide behind the Mirror.

As they eat they take on form,
Evolving as they feed;
Our nightmares give them substance,
Our fears a place to breed.

Growing ever stronger,
While we forget our past;
They hunger now for flesh and blood,
From just beyond the glass.

BEDTIME STORIES FOR NAUGHTY CHILDREN

So if you can't recall your dreams,
When you wake from your sleep;
Perhaps the Eaters came last night,
While you were snoring deep.

Perhaps you wake each morning,
And gaze into the mirror;
To comb your hair and brush your teeth,
While taunting your worst fears.

They peer back ever anxious,
While you are unaware;
Their fangs dripping with venom,
Death waiting in their stare.

For in the deep, dark, chasm,
Just behind the glass;
An ageless malice lingers,
From the shadows of the past.

One day they'll rise in anger,
From the vast black void beyond;
To sate their lust and cruel hate,
And mankind will be gone.

They'll reach out from the mirror,
Clawing at your heart;
The Eaters of Dreams will rise up,
And tear your soul apart.

Their comfort is our funeral pyre,
Their bloodlust is our doom;
And even now they stare at you,
In every mirrored room.

Scarlet Pastures

Like dew upon the petals,
Of a rose kissed by the dawn,
And the cool, crisp breath of Autumn,
In the fields of Escalon;
Crimson droplets glisten,
On the flesh of murdered men,
Whose sightless eyes stare greeting,
Dawn's glowing birth again.

Excerpt from the *Steedman Scrolls*

The Eaters Of
Ashes

Sit down children, I have a tale to tell,
For 'Tis that time of year;
When we celebrate Thanksgiving,
Because Halloween draws near.

You've all heard of the Headless Horseman,
And of Sleepy Hollow's plight;
But there are far more dreadful
and loathsome things,
That live in the dead of the night.

For daylight was intended for mortals,
For children and women and men;
For singing, dancing and pleasure,
While the sun smiles warmly on them.

But there are creatures that dwell in darkness,
They rise once you've snuffed out the lights;
They wake as the shadows grow longer,
Creeping close, lurking just out of sight.

Such monsters have always been near us,
Feeding once we've went to sleep;
They were born in the first Age of Chaos,
In a place that the sun's never seen.

In caverns no light ever lighted,
Far deeper than the black pits of Hel;
Malcontent, malice and hatred,
Lend them a sulphurous smell.

Craving the flesh of the living,
They slither from under your bed;
Peering from half-open closets,
Waiting till you turn your head.

Once these dread spirits were shapeless,
Before the great folly of Cain;
But Solomon learned of their secrets,
It was he who discovered their names.

Long ago men knew the power,
That resides in the knowing of names;
But the Dark Ages robbed many memories,
And twisted the world with its pain.

Knowing a name gives one power,
To conjure and summon a thing;
Performed in the auspicious hour,
You can call forth almost anything.

There lived a young peasant named Stephen,
He and his parents were poor;
Eating just stale bread and corn husks,
Thrown away by the family next door.

One day while exploring a meadow,
He discovered an ancient old tomb;
The headstone was broken and crumbling,
Inscribed with a warning of doom.

But Stephen did not heed the warning,
Graven by skilled pagan hands;
When even the wise men were fearful,
Of the things they did not understand.

An Age when mankind were the hunted,
And Shadows crept over the land;
When hideous beasts stalked the living,
An Age now forgotten by man.

Poor Stephen thought only of treasure,
Perhaps buried somewhere below;
He dug with a pick and a shovel,
Till at last with the sun sinking low;

His blade struck on something more solid,
Deep in the black, musky loam;
A sarcophagus curiously crafted,
Chiselled from smooth, solid stone.

Stephen was wild with excitement,
And quickly smashed open the cask;
Inside lay a skeletal figure,
With a scroll clenched tight in it's grasp.

BEDTIME STORIES FOR NAUGHTY CHILDREN

A green vapour hissed from the coffin,
Swirling about the young lad;
Making him dizzy and nauseous,
Like nothing before ever had.

Grim laughter ripped though the darkness,
Shadows swarmed in like a plague;
He sank to his knees in the cool earth,
Sensing the mistake he had made.

Visions of horrors assailed him,
A blasphemous voice called his name;
Then the strange mist paled and vanished,
And his thoughts once again became sane.

Disappointed in finding no treasure,
He snatched up the mouldering scroll;
He would sell it somewhere at the market,
To whom though he did not yet know.

Returning at last to his hovel,
Stephen lay down for the night;
But the prize he'd uncovered intrigued him,
In the flickering hearth-fire light.

He carefully unrolled the parchment,
The writing was strange and obscene;
Scribed by the Black wizard Therion,
In an era that now was a dream.

Slowly he traced every figure,
With his fingertips one at a time;
And the meaning of each magick sigal,
Began to unfold in his mind.

The fire glared lurid and brightly,
The flames leaping hungrily now;
The words captivated his senses,
Understanding without knowing how.

A voice spoke from deep in the shadows,
In the dark at the edge of the room;
It urged him to read out the writing,
In the cold silver light of the Moon.

Stephen complied without thinking,
Some strange force possessing his soul;
He put on his worn boots and jacket,
And hastily snatched up the scroll.

The Moon was a sickle-shaped crescent,
The stars gleamed like jewels on high;
As he called out arcane incantations,
To the lost souls that wander the night.

His voice took on inhuman timbre,
Like the clang of an old iron bell;
Resounding across hills and valleys,
It was heard in the dark bowels of Hell.

Then came the rushing of ghost wind,
Up from the mist-shrouded marsh;
Witch-fire sprang up in a circle,
As he stood there alone in the dark.

Something had perceived his summons,
And even now answered the call;
A grey haze rushed toward him like plague flies,
On a battlefield late in the fall.

A gaunt visage took shape before him,
Its features contorted and grim;
Yellow eyes smouldering thinly,
It peered now intently at him.

No nightmare both real or imagined,
Could rival the lad's dread and fear;
The ghoul spoke in low, bestial fashion,
In a tone few but demons can hear.

"We are the Eaters of Ashes,
We feed upon dead martyr's bones;
We answer the call of our Master,
And rise from our cursed abode."

"No other voice brings us hither,
Save for The One with the Key;
Bound by our oath to the Black Scroll,
Anxious to once more be free."

"So now we do stand here before thee,
Awaiting thy final request;
Fulfill now thy part of the bargain;
We hunger for innocent flesh."

The young lad stood frozen in terror,
At the sight of the spectres he'd raised;
The Eaters of Ashes grew restless,
Piercing his soul with their gaze.

The ghost leader drew ever closer,
And poor Stephen screamed in alarm;
Sensing their growing suspicion,
Fearing their vengeance and harm.

At long last he gathered his courage,
As the legion of phantom's looked on;
Instinctively knowing that spirits,
Could not stand the red light of dawn.

"I'm just a boy from the village",
Said Stephen as best as he could;
"I know nothing of wizards and witchcraft;
And I would take back those words if I could."

"I discovered this scroll in the meadow,
I pried it from skeletal hands;
If the man in the tomb was your Master,
Then take up your troubles with him."

"Nay!" cried the now angered spirit,
"'Tis thee who hast called, and we came!
Though your features are ever more youthful,
Than The One who once knew us by name."

"Nonetheless thou hast wielded the Black Scroll,
As only an adept could do;
So I say that thy name must be Therion,
And demand that thou give us our due."

"Long have we suffered in darkness,
The dead men from under the sea;
If thou wilt not hold up the bargain,
Then surrender the Black Scroll to me."

"If I am to do now as you bid me,"
The trembling boy answered the ghoul;
"You must swear that you will not mistreat me,
Nor persist that I give you your due."

"I yet smell the stench of a mage here,"
Growled the spirit in bitter reply;
"Yet shall I grant thee this parlay,
And swear that your soul shall not die."

Stephen felt much more relieved then,
And handed the spirit the scroll;
The Demon grinned grim satisfaction,
And bade his dark legion to go.

Then he turned swiftly on Stephen,
And snatched up the lad by his hair;
The boy cried out, "Please do not hurt me!
"You promised me you would be fair!"

"I be no servant of mortals,"
Replied the phantasm with glee;
"You made your fatal mistake, boy,
When you decided to bargain with me!"

"The Black Scroll was your protection,
It has kept us at bay these long years;
Now be kind, lad, and do me a favour;
Scream while I savour your tears."

So it was that young Stephen was murdered,
By the Eaters of Ashes that night;
His pale flesh and bones torn to pieces,
In the crimson of dawns early light.

But still to this day north of Scotland,
As the mist rolls in thick on the breeze;
You can hear the faint cries of poor Stephen,
In his grave somewhere under the seas.

Lament

My soul is torn in torment
My heart sundered by pain
The light that gleamed so brightly
Now never shall again!

The Eaters Of The Dead

Once I was a young man,
In a keep of carven stone;
Set high upon a limestone hill,
As pale as dead men's bones.

Ten thousand legions had I then,
In helms of hammered steel;
With archers, knights, and pike-men,
Like locust at my heel.

My kingdom was a peaceful realm,
It stretched out to the sea;
My countrymen were peasant folk,
Content with being free.

Then came the Christians marching,
A black swarm from the east;
Cruel as the devil's laughter,
They spread like a disease.

Men, women, and children fell,
Before their swords and spears;
And Pagan soil ran red with blood,
Amid their heartless jeers.

They marched into my kingdom,
Like soulless death machines;
The infirm and old they slaughtered,
In hungry guillotines.

The young disembowelled and butchered,
The women raped and killed;
The men impaled and suffering,
On stakes across the hills.

My wrath was greatly kindled,
At the horror of their ways;
And I swore before the Pagan gods,
My vengeance on that day.

I gathered up my armies,
And rode across the plains;
On a mighty stallion black as death,
In a coat of fine mesh chain.

My country was a ruin,
My people all but gone;
I'd just my sword and army,
And hate to drive me on.

At first we heard their voices,
Singing songs of doom;
They praised their dying god-man,
In the morning's misty gloom.

Then at last we saw them,
Like sands beside the sea;
Shouting bloody triumph,
'Till they caught sight of me.

We halted in formation,
Prepared to meet our deaths;
With a curse against their hellish god,
Upon our dying breaths.

Their general rode to meet us,
His lips a grisly grin;
They outnumbered us like plague flies,
These butchers of our kin.

"Surrender!" He demanded,
"In the name of Jesus Christ;
And we'll commit thy souls with mercy,
To the depths of Hell this night."

I stared back at the madman,
And laughed into his face;
"This day," said I, "You shall meet your god,
For you will never leave this place."

"You've conquered every nation,
In the name of your bloody Lord;
But so too did the Catholics,
And the Muslim hordes before."

"And as you now, they too did stand,
Upon this very place;
Demanding my surrender,
With sword and spear and mace."

"But I refused, as even now,
And cursed them all to Hell;
I slew their armies to a man,
And I'll slay thee as well."

"So call upon your god of Death,
Who rules men's hearts with fear;
Entreat the awesome terrors,
Of this saviour you hold dear."

"But know that this is Pagan soil,
Your home is far away;
Soon you'll find your god is blind,
And deaf upon this day."

"The voices of my ancestors,
Now call upon the wind;
As I pray to gods whose very name,
You deem to be a sin."

"I invoke the ancient powers,
Of Earth and Sea and Sky;
They wake and wait my summons,
To rally at my side."

With that the general rode away,
To prepare his men for war;
He cursed our Gods and Country,
As he'd done each day before.

First trumpets blared and drums beat deep,
Across the great expanse;
Then everything was deathly still,
As we prepared to dance.

Their knights drew up to lead the charge,
And archers plied their bows;
The sky grew black with feathered shafts,
And we fell before our foes.

Then came the shrill, unearthly screams,
As men writhed in the dirt;
My archers loosed at my command,
And Christian cries were heard.

As if as one, both armies closed,
With knights leading the way;
A steel torrent of pounding hooves,
As madness swept the fray.

Swords and axes rose and fell,
Smashing skulls and shields;
And Hell reaped souls in endless droves,
But we refused to yield.

Our enemies would not relent,
Consumed by lust and greed;
I knew our strength would soon be spent,
If we did not concede.

I know not now how long I fought,
But soon my men were slain;
I stood alone and faced my foes,
A Pagan, gone insane.

My sword was like a whirlwind,
It sang a song of death;
I staggered on, my strength near gone,
And fought like one possessed.

They'd counted on surrender,
But they had counted wrong;
I dared their god to kill me,
As I leapt into the throng.

Then suddenly the Earth and Sky,
Were shaken violently;
And thunder crashed as lightening flashed,
At everything but me.

From somewhere far beyond the Sky,
Burning brimstone fell;
The blood-soaked Earth split open wide,
The gaping maw of Hell.

The Christians fled for cover,
Their general shook with fright;
As demons rose from dark abodes,
To aid me in my fight.

I still recall their desperate cries,
As monstrous things rushed in;
To cleanse the world of Christian hate,
And wipe away their sins.

At last the plain was empty,
For none survived but me;
I thanked the ancient Powers,
And turned at last to leave.

T'was then I spied the general,
Bleeding out his last;
A crippled, ruined, wreckage,
Now dying in the grass.

"What black arts have you, Pagan?"
He stammered painfully;
"To conjure up the legions,
Of Hell to fight with me?"

"I have no special power,"
I quietly replied;
"I'm just a simple Pagan,
With justice by my side."

"My kinfolk were the Keepers,
Of this land you sought to own;
For ages we have guarded it,
And made this country home."

"Our ancient rites protect Her,
From famine, drought, and harm;
Our dead live on forever,
In the Black loam of Her arms."

Then the general's eyes bulged out,
His face a mask of dread;
And from the chasm specters rose,
The Eaters of the Dead.

Their eyes were glowing embers,
Their features wreathed in flame;
The ones who rule the caverns,
Where demons go insane.

Their teeth were sharp as razors,
Dripping putrid slime;
Their bodies vile and monstrous,
Too frightening to define.

Serpents sprouted from their necks,
Writhing in the air;
Their breath reeked rotting corpses,
Too sickening to bear.

They reached out for the general,
Grasping at his leg;
Their fingers gripped like talons,
To drag him to his grave.

I heard the general screaming,
As they tore him apart;
Somewhere down in the darkness,
They feasted on his heart.

Now I am an old man,
But I still recall that day;
When Hell unleashed its fury,
And my homeland was saved.

Fear

You gather every Sunday,
To sing your rusted hymns;
And beg to be forgiven,
For all your secret sins.

Offering up your bloodstained prayers,
Like shards of broken glass;
Intoned from memory, Etched in boredom,
Dredged up from the past.

Kneeling at the altar,
Your god-man hangs above;
Portrayed in pain and torment,
Why should he show you love?

You keep him nailed up on a cross!
Thorns wreathing his head;
A mask of pain and horror,
Bleeding, dying, dead!

Spikes drove deep, fingers splayed,
Features stained by tears;
A grisly, tortured memory,
Now worshiped out of fear.

Fear that Hell is waiting,
Fear that you will die;
Fear that you are being watched,
By cruel, infernal eyes.

Fear that those you've slaughtered,
The witches, saints, and poor;
Will one day rise from history,
And pound upon your door.

Fear that you are guilty,
Of mankind's greatest lies;
Fear your god won't save you,
From all that you despise.

Fear the truth is waiting,
Fear cause you're a fraud;
Fear you've slain in Jesus name,
And mocked your loving god!

The Cave of Baell-rean

There's a cave in the heart of the snow-covered Alps,
In a region once drank by the sea;
Its gaping mouth crusted in sharp icy spikes,
High up on a mist-shrouded peak.
Not since the days of the Kings of the North,
And the first Queen of old Isaheim,
Have men seen its fanged maw nor stepped foot inside,
The entrance to the Cave of Baell-rean.

Once it looked out on vineyards and groves,
That painted the deep valleys green;
And the old Sacred Tree grew just near its mouth,
A tree like no other since seen.
Even before snow had buried it deep,
Under ice in this lofty domain;
Few were the men who dared venture within,
And those who lived came back insane.

But once in my youth I climbed that dread peak,
On a bitterly cold winter's day;
I scaled up the ice falls and sheer jagged cliffs,
Carving handholds each step of the way.
The wind howled with furious hatred and ire,
In a blizzard of hailstones and sleet;
Yet I would not turn back from the great granite spire,
That men once called Uriel's Keep.

I felt its contempt and its ominous dread,
Long before I at last spied the door;
And I paused by the petrified stump of Yggdrasill,
The Great Ash my kinsmen adored.
Before me loomed Baell-rean, a stark, empty void,
Its frigid jaws beckoning me;
Cold tongues of thick fog rose up from within,
Like dragon's breath spewn at my knees.

I cursed at the darkness and sparked up a torch,
It sputtered and then flared to life;
And drawing my sword, I stepped through the door,
As Baell-rean's black shrank back from my light.
To my horror I saw now in heaps on the floor,
A grisly and terrible sight;
The corpses of those who had come here before,
Their courage had cost them their lives.

Past the ruins of creatures and beasts long extinct,
I carefully moved on ahead;
Amid the shattered remains of strange, nameless things,
That feed on the flesh of the dead.
The air burned my nostrils and made my eyes sting,
Reeking of death and disease;
I gripped my sword tightly and covered my face,
As the stench became too vile to breathe.

Finding a stairway carved into the stone,
I spiralled down in the abyss;
Traversing wide chasms and red molten flows,
Where deadly steam spurted and hissed.
Shapeless forms lurked ever near in the shadows,
Cruel eyes glowed red all around;
Dead spirits haunted each perilous step,
And a drum somewhere started to pound.

Downward I went, passing graveyards of Dwarves,
The stone steps now crumbling away;
Huge spiders leapt out from cracks in the walls,
Where cobwebs hung matted and grey.
Passages branched to the left and the right,
Some piled high with white, broken bones;
The victims of Goblins and great cavern Trolls,
Their skulls smashed with huge, bloodstained stones.

The darkness resounded with hideous mirth,
My pathway was leading to Hell;
I knew unseen devils were watching with glee,
But from where yet I just couldn't tell.
I know not how long I delved through the black maze,
I lost track of hours and days;
But at last when I came to the chamber I sought,
A hideous fiend blocked my way.

It's features a blasphemous mockery of life,
A nightmare no sane mind could dream;
I knew every carcass that littered this cave,
Had been victims of this dreadful Thing.
It was spawned in the dim dawn of Earth long ago,
In the ooze of primordial seas;
More lives had It claimed
than the Bubonic Plague,
And now It glared anxious at me.

For thousands of years It had waited below,
Hungry for fresh, tender meat;
Consumed by It's lust for souls dripping in blood,
But no one had come to Baell-rean.
From deep, sunken sockets It's black oily eyes,
Glimmered with unholy greed;
It's slavering jaws quivered, opening wide;
I'd be damned if this Thing would eat me!

It lashed out with tentacles covered in spikes,
And long talons tore at my skin;
I slashed at the demon, unwilling to yield,
As primeval hate welled up within.
My blade severed cartilage, tendons and bone,
And still the Thing would not relent;
I fought like a madman, possessed and insane,
With the last of my strength nearly spent.

My blade found its mark on the nightmare's thick skull,
Splitting It's head scalp to teeth;
It staggered away and then slumped to the floor,
And no Heaven or Black Hell beneath;
Has witnessed such fury and ungodly rage,
As I vengefully hacked off It's head;
Then I climbed up it's scaled chest and cut out It's heart,
Making sure the goddamned Thing was dead.

Gasping for breath now I slung off the gore,
That clung to my battle-notched blade;
Then I moved past the demon and stepped through a door,
A portal no human had made.
Within sprawled a chamber that arched high and wide,
A vault chiselled into the stone;
The malachite floor tiles were covered in dust,
From an Age that had long come and gone.

In the midst of the room stood an ivory altar,
A tiered dais rose just beyond;
Upon it had been placed a great amber throne,
That glowed like the smouldering dawn.
With a dagger I'd made from a meteorite,
I carefully cut my own wrist;
As my blood stained the altar a blue witch-fire rose,
Consuming my dark crimson gift.

Then all of a sudden a vision appeared,
On the seat on the shimmering throne;
With luminous brightness She blinded my eyes,
And I knew I'd regret what I'd done.
The silence was shattered by the sound of a voice,
It rang like a crystalline bell;
"I am Lamashtu, and this was my home,
Before it was turned into Hell."

"Once I was worshipped and loved by the world,
Once the whole Earth was my home;
But soon men forgot me, and darkness closed in,
And I was shut up here alone.
Long ages passed as I wept tears of blood,
For no one remembered my name;
When I was forgotten, my power grew weak,
And soon all my enemies came."

"With curses too foul and profane to recount,
My nemesis shackled me here;
Then slowly Shamash desecrated the things,
That I had held sacred and dear.
Every so often, as the centuries stole by,
I felt mortal footsteps come close;
But none came to free me——all fled, all gone;
And with them my last desperate hopes.

"At last out of anger I conjured my will,
The last of my magick and might;
I summoned the creature that stood at my door,
A demon of shadow and night.
I charged him to slay everything in this cave,
And he followed my orders with glee;
But now you have come here and killed him this night,
And in doing so you've set me free."

"Free from the prison in which I was kept,
Free from this cold, lonely cell;
Free from the horror that lurked at my door,
For it turned my revenge into Hell.
It trapped me alone here when men came no more,
When nothing else lived in Baell-rean;
Now you have freed me to live in your world,
And Oh! What a slaughter there'll be!"

"For all of my power and all of my strength,
Will soon be restored unto me;
Once you've returned to your home in the east,
And spoken to others of Me.
I need only a few to discover my name,
Just a handful who truly believe;
To awaken my might and replenish my strength;
Woe to those who forgot about me!"

Upon hearing these words I was stricken with fright,
And fled from Baell-rean straight away;
I have never returned, my lesson is learned,
But Lamashtu remains to this day.
She stands by my bedside, She lurks at my back,
Urging me always to speak;
To tell of the cave of Baell-rean where I found her,
And cause someone else to believe.

Soon I will die and be buried at last,
With all the mistakes that I've made;
But I fear some poor wretch might discover the path,
That leads to Lamashtu's black cave.
So I've written my tale as a warning of doom,
God pity the world on the day;
That the cave of Baell-rean is discovered again,
And some fool speaks Lamashtu's dread name!

The Raven
and
The Dove

I dreamed we were together
In serpentine embrace
You looked like an angel
In cold, white, ashen lace
We danced until the stars burned out
As heaven swirled above
No forgiveness for our sins
The raven and the dove.

I dreamed we were together
And I fallen from grace
All my tender kisses
Now scarred upon your face
My proud wings burnt to cinders
Amid the molten blaze
Bloody tears shed freely
In burning brimstone haze.

I loved you ever dearly
Caressing you within
You never should have suffered me
To stain you with my sin
Now I'm lost in darkness
Still groping for that love
My eternal torment
The raven and the dove.

I dreamed we were together
It was the sweetest dream
The memory of it haunts me
I wish I still had wings
To fly back up to heaven
To steal just one last kiss
To savour your aroma
And die at last in bliss.

Instead I wander blindly
In caverns dark and deep
My heart and soul still longing
But never finding peace
Searching in the shadows
Dreaming of your face
Empty, broken, hopeless
Lost without a trace.

Does the dove remember?
Will she ever dream of me?
Will she someday feel my torment,
And yearn to set me free?
Or must I live forever
In this cursed and wretched place
Sustained by just a memory
Of her kisses and her face.

Rust

Had I the words to whisper
The strength to speak my pain
The will to suffer longer
The tears to cry in vain

Id tell thee all my torments
And rise up from this dust
This hollow hell, this grave of grief
This endless, aching rust.

The Fairie Rhyme

There is a land that only Fairies see;
Beneath the moss and roots of forest trees;
Hidden under brush and fallen leaves;
Protected by the wild Bumble Bees.

In groves of Oak and Pine in rugged lands;
Where the first of Elvish altars stands;
If you scrape the leaves back with your hands;
You'll find a door embedded in the sand.

Graven on that door you will then see;
An ancient rhyme in runes-----that is the key;
No human tongue has voiced those words but me;
I learned then from the wild Bumble Bees.

Lady slippers grow about the door;
Above the graves of those that live no more;
Fairies who were once slain in a war;
When men rose up against a Goblin horde.

If thou fain would know the magick spell;
Ye must please the bees or they won't tell;
With sweetened water drawn from sacred well;
That lies within the Dead Land of Muspell.

Once

Once I had the truest friend
No other shall I find
Within this life or those to come
Nor those I've left behind

Whose trust was ever constant
Whose love was ever long
Whose faith was so unflinching
Whose courage ever strong

I've shed a hundred thousand tears
I'll shed them all again
For every cherished memory
Until I meet my end.

In memory of Laren Michael James Petryshyn---RIP

The Withered Tree

There's a desolate road that few now know
Near the place where I was born
It leads to a graveyard where briars grow
Forgotten and forlorn.

Beside it stands an ancient tree
Where crows and ravens rest
Its branches grey and withered
Like the skin on a dead man's chest.

Mandrakes blossom within its shade
Beneath its twisted limbs
From which were once hung murderers
In penance for their sins.

A thousand years of winter
And searing summer heat
The tree has stood there silent
It's thick roots going deep.

Down into the Black Earth
To the very bowels of Hell
To drink the blood of angels
The Chosen Ones who fell.

XPƐ⊓⊃ ⅂ Ɛ⊓℧◌⅃⊃

Memoirs of a Dying King

My dreams smoulder to ashes,
Warm summers burnt to dusk;
My shinning helm of youthful spring,
Now lies riven in rust.
My hopes depart unbidden,
Leaves borne by Autumn wind;
Dark shadows slowly lengthen,
As Winter's chill creeps in.

——The Chronicles of King Xalton

BEDTIME STORIES FOR NAUGHTY CHILDREN

Ephigy

Burn this husk to ash and dust
This hollow, sallow shell
It toiled with bitter tears in life
I'll need it not in Hell!

For wine has lost its flavour
The night grows dark and long
The flame has glut the taper
The light will soon be gone.

What use have I of heartache?
What lesson shall I learn?
I've not the will to linger
Nor shall I soon return!

The Fiend

Last night when I went to bed,
Darkness filled my room;
I lay there staring all around,
It felt more like my tomb.
Outside the wind howled like a banshee,
Moonlight filtered in;
I watched my closet door creak open,
Shadows stirred within.

Black monstrous fingers grasping,
On the pale white closet door;
Claws gleaming like polished glass,
Scratched against the floor.
Slowly something hideous
Crept out from the dark,
Its features grim and twisted,
Eyes glowing bright and stark.

'Twas not the angel sent by god,
To give me pleasant dreams;
The one my mother promised,
Was no where to be seen.
This was something evil,
Of that I had no doubt;
My heart raced as its wretched face,
Peered menacingly about.

It flew across my bedroom,
In one gigantic leap;
It's laughter was demonic,
It's hairy body reeked.
I gasped for air amid the stench,
Of sulphurous decay;
Knowing it would torment me,
Until the break of day.

I shall never sleep again,
Nor spend the night alone;
I fear that it will soon return,
To rend my flesh and bones.
It's loathsome face still haunts me,
Even in the day;
I cannot escape it,
And it won't go away.

The Black Star

Once a star lit up the sky
A silver spike of doom
It pierced the night, a jewelled thorn
On the breast of the Maiden Moon.

I was a simple heathen then
A peaceful pagan soul
I saw the star of dread that night
And heard my death bell toll.

Eastern mages saw it too
And followed from afar
Seeking to appease the gods
That sent the grim, bright star.

Gifts they brought on camels
Over icy plains
Through dessert wastes and molten winds
And freezing mountain rains.

The gods disdained their precious bribes
The mages met their fate
Their heads impaled on iron pikes
Outside the city gate.

Predicted in forbidden books
Of magick dark and grim
The star that blazed across the sky
Would bring about the end.

A zealot child was born the night
That black star marred the sky
A revolutionary martyr
Condemned at birth to die.

They hung him from an ancient tree
And thrust spears in his side
He cried and gasped and bled all night
And finally he died.

A few devoted madmen
Took him down at dawn
They hid his body in a tomb
From the eyes of men and god.

Soon a new religion
Spread throughout the land
Hailing a new era
Of peace for every man.

They decried our heathen gods
And shunned our pagan ways
We fed them to the lions
And sent them to their graves.

'Till a zealot ruler
Seized the crown and throne
He outlawed every heathen
And smashed our hopes and homes.

We became the hunted
The butchered, skinned and flayed
They killed our men and raped our wives
And burned them at the stake.

We fled from every city
Across the swamps and plains
Back into the ancient groves
That still bore pagan names.

The forest gave us shelter
And there we lived in peace
Safe from fear and terror
Beneath the solemn trees.

The world outside our forest
Became a wretched place
Bloody wars and terrors
The sword, the rack, the mace;

Kingdoms burned to ashes
Empires rose and fell
God kings stalked the trembling lands
And reaped the world for hell.

I curse the night that Black Star
Glimmered up on high
And the hellish gods that sent it
To slash across the sky!

Hail, Tiamat!
I hear thee whisper in the night;
Hail, long lost Sister of our Sacred Mother,
Messenger of woe and blight!
What perils and dread await us,
When thy fires light the sky?
When the children of men flee to the mountains,
And beg the gods to let them die?
Yet if we might find some small grace within thy sight,
Look upon us with kindness,
And have mercy on that dread night.

Communion

You waited up there patient all along
You charmed my soul like a serpent with a song
Now I'm finally past the point of no return
But I've never felt at peace like this
I was enraptured in the darkness of your kiss
I was enthralled within the shadows of your bliss
And now I plunge into forever on your lips
As midnight shrouds us in this cloak of stars.

Rise Again

Day is coming to an end now
Night falls silent all around
Doesn't this world seem so peaceful
When viewed from underground?
My mother left some flowers
My father said a silent prayer
While friends and lovers mourn my memory
The one I love will soon be here;
So lay me down beside an oak tree
Pillow my head upon a stone
Hide my eyes underneath pennies
Scatter roses o'er my bones
Blanket me under the cool earth
With a spade in sheets of loam;

I'll rise again.

Immaculate Conception

Through love and lust was I conceived
When passion's flame gave life to seed
And I, in spirit, yet agreed,
When love by lust was first perceived.

I came not from some mythic guph
Nor some heavenly abode above
No stork nor pale white little dove
But from the stars and borne of love
Conveyed by lust born out of love
And thus was I born out of love.

Your ancient saint's and prophet's postulation
Divine words spake our grand creation
Bear no sway on my persuasion
The bud of lust gave bloom to love and copulation.

And I yet in another space
A plane where time was out of place
Gleaned the future brilliance of my mother's face
And deigned to live the love and lust of mortal race
So coalesced within the womb of their embrace.

Thank-you for buying my book!!!

I sincerely hope you hope you have enjoyed reading these strange tales as much as I have enjoyed writing and conveying them to you. If this book has bored you, burn it. Never breathe another word to a living soul. If, however, my words have entertained you and touched some special place within your soul...or even better, disturbed it...please tell everyone you know.

Azriel St. Michael

Merry meet
Merry part
Merry meet again!

Azriel St. Michael

www.azrielstmichael.com

WWW.AUDIOPORNMUSIC.COM

Check out the video for "Sweet 16"
by Azriel St. Michael AND Audio Porn on
You Tube, Vevo and Netshows.
Become a fan of Azriel on Facebook and get
all the latest news and updates first.
Also be sure to check out the Facebook page for this book as well!!!
Post your picture with the book on the wall and
tell the world how much you enjoyed it!

----Fan Mail----
Azriel St. Michael
RR5 Site 17 Comp 49
Prince Albert, Sk
Canada
S6v-5R3

Born in Norfolk, Viriginia, Azriel St. Michael moved to Canada with his parents as a child. He wrote his first short story at the age of ten. After graduating high school, he joined several rock bands and traveled throughout Canada and the USA playing guitar and singing.

In 2006 he founded the Saskatoon-based rock band *Jezebels Kiss* along with drummer *Byron Black*. From 2006 to 2011 *Jezebels Kiss* performed over 450 shows across Western Canada.

Without You (The Necrophiliac's Love Song) was featured in the movie *Checkmate* by Prime Factor Films in Atlanta, Ga. The complete soundtrack is available through CD Baby.com.

Let Me Go was featured on an album titled *Just Rock!* Released by Moiko Records in support of Habitat for Humanity.

In November 2011 Azriel joined Toronto's *Black Sun* as lead singer and co-writer. Their debut album *Edge of Darkness* is slated for a March, 2013 release.

In 2012, Azriel and producer / *Hydrogyn* guitarist Jeff Westlake teamed up with former *Jezebels Kiss* drummer Byron Black to form a new group, the result of which became *Audio Porn*. *Audio Porn's* debut album was released in Europe, the UK, and North America in August 2012 via Music Buy Mail and Super D distribution on JK Records.

Azriel is presently working on a new album with *Audio Porn*. Fans can expect the release in 2013.

For more information check out the band's official site, www.audiopornmusic.com.

Azriel St. Michael is endorsed by Knucklehead Guitar Strings and uses them exclusively.

Demand the music of Audio Porn and Black Sun on your local rock radio to-day!!!

Coming soon from Shemyaza Press and Azriel St. Michael

LYRICS FOR A DYING WORLD

BLOOD AND GLORY

LEGEND OF THE BLOODY GRAIL

JK Entertainment Canada
JK Records
Shemyaza Press

SHEMYAZA PRESS

A DIVISION OF THE SHEMYAZA SYNDICATE GROUP